W9-AOK-349

WITHDRAWN

THE PRINCE AND THE SPHINX

A RETELLING BY CARI MEISTER   ILLUSTRATED BY LEONARDO MESCHINI

PICTURE WINDOW BOOKS
a capstone imprint

🪲 CAST OF CHARACTERS

Thutmose IV (THUT-mose): an Egyptian king who uncovered Khafra's Great Sphinx

Sendji (SEND-jee): Thutmose's pet lion cub

Sennefur (SEN-if-fur) twins: Thutmose's friends

Harmachis (har-MAH-cheez): god of the rising sun

Khafra (KAF-rah): an Egyptian king who built the second Giza pyramid and the Great Sphinx

🪲 WORDS TO KNOW

chariot—a lightweight, two-wheeled cart pulled by horses

destiny—the events that will necessarily happen to a certain person or thing in the future

Dream Stele—a stone slab that Thutmose IV placed near the Great Sphinx to tell of his vision of Harmachis, and his rise to power

faith—trust in and support for someone

Pyramids of Giza—triangular structures built by the Egyptians in Giza to hold the bodies of dead kings

pharaoh—a king of ancient Egypt

temple—a building that is used for the worshipping of gods or a god

IN A LONG-AGO TIME OF ANCIENT EGYPTIAN KINGS AND GODS,

there lived a prince named Thutmose IV. For as long as Thutmose could remember, his brothers had been angry with him. They knew Thutmose was their father's favorite son. And they feared that one day their father would make Thutmose king. So the brothers often plotted against Thutmose. But Thutmose longed for their friendship, and this made his heart heavy.

One hot afternoon Thutmose raced his chariot across the sand. He stopped in front of the temple and ran up the steps. He knelt before the gods and prayed, "Great Egyptian gods of my grandfathers, thank you for your kindness. Help prepare me to be a great leader. But most importantly, please calm my brothers' anger toward me."

The gods heard Thutmose's requests, and they had great faith in him. They put a plan into motion.

The next morning Thutmose woke very early. Everyone was asleep, even the servants.

The stone floor felt cool on his bare feet as he rose from bed. But he loved the chill of morning. He knew that later in the day, the hot desert sun would beat down on him.

Thutmose's pet lion cub, Sendji, heard him wake. She yawned and licked her paws. It was only last week that Thutmose had rescued her from a hungry crocodile. Even so, Sendji was fiercely attached to her newfound father.

"Good morning, Sendji," Thutmose whispered. "You can come with me. But you must be quiet and not wake the others."

The young cub padded close behind Thutmose as he left the royal bedchamber.

Thutmose quietly left the royal home and walked down the sandy path to where his friends, the Sennefur twins, lived. He stood outside the window. "Good morning!" he whispered. "It looks like a great morning for hunting. Let's leave before anyone wakes."

The prince and his friends grabbed four of the fastest horses. They found two of the lightest chariots from the royal yard and sped away.

Nothing lightened the Prince's heart more than hunting. He laughed and joked with his friends all morning as they chased antelope. But soon the desert sun grew too hot for hunting.

By this time the trio had traveled quite far. Thutmose knew they must be close to the Pyramids of Giza.

"My friends," he said, "will you please wait here for me? I wish to offer up my prayers to the mighty god Harmachis at the pyramids."

The brothers agreed. Then Thutmose and Sendji disappeared into the vast ocean of sand.

Soon Thutmose saw the pyramids in the distance. "WHOA!" he yelled to stop his sweaty horses.

Thutmose stared at the gigantic structures. He had heard about them before, but he had never seen them up close.

"They're magnificent!" he cried. He fell to his knees in prayer.

Thutmose let his horses rest for a moment, but he could not resist the pyramids. Soon he and his horses were speeding toward them.

By now it was midday, and it was hot. Thutmose left his horses and began to walk. As Thutmose neared the pyramids, he saw something sticking up from the sand. "Harmachis!" said Thutmose.

It was indeed a statue made to honor Harmachis, the god of the rising sun. The statue's face was that of the pharaoh Khafra. Its lion body was buried in sand.

"Great god of the rising sun, you are strong and powerful. I thank you for your many blessings," said Thutmose. "Please protect me as I rest in the shade of your mighty face."

Thutmose lay down, but he did not sleep, for something above him rumbled. The ground beneath him started to tremble.

13

Thutmose looked up. He couldn't believe what he saw!

The head of the great rock Sphinx moved. Its eyes blinked and stared right at Thutmose. Then the great statue spoke. "Do not be afraid, Thutmose," it said. "I am Harmachis, god of the rising sun, and the father of all pharaohs. I have been watching you since you were a small boy. You are strong and courageous, wise and learned. But most important, you respect Egypt's gods.

"Do not let your heart be heavy," the statue continued. "Your brothers will soon ask for your forgiveness for treating you cruelly. They will see that it is your destiny to rule Egypt. You will be one of the greatest pharaohs of all time. My blessings will be upon you, and you shall live a long and successful life. But you must promise me one thing."

Thutmose bowed before the statue. "I will do as you ask," he said.

Harmachis blinked and spoke again. "Very good, my son. Right now all you can see of this great statue is my head. Over the years sand has covered my body and mighty paws. Please clear away the sand, so that people can once again see me and worship me."

When Thutmose agreed, a great blinding light filled the sky, and he collapsed.

18

When the prince woke, night had come. "I've been asleep for hours," Thutmose said as he stroked Sendji's soft ears. "I had the strangest dream ... no, it wasn't a dream, was it?"

Sendji roared her tiny roar at the mighty Sphinx statue.

Thutmose looked up. The statue was as still as stone. "I must go find my friends and tell them what happened!" he said.

Thutmose gathered his horses and sped back across the desert to the Sennefur twins.

"Thutmose!" the twins exclaimed as he woke them from their sleep. "You have returned! We feared that something evil had happened to you!"

Thutmose smiled. "No, it was quite the opposite," he said. Thutmose told them of his vision of Harmachis.

Immediately the two brothers fell at his feet and worshipped him. They knew that the great god Harmachis had spoken.

Thutmose, Sendji, and the Sennefur twins returned to the palace. From that day forward, Thutmose was blessed by the gods.

It was not long before Thutmose was declared pharaoh. His own brothers bowed before him. "Good brother," they said, "we are sorry for how we have treated you. Please forgive us."

Thutmose accepted their apologies with a happy heart.

"And now," Thutmose told his people, "I will keep my promise to the god of the rising sun. Tomorrow a large group of men will start uncovering the Great Sphinx statue of Khafra."

In the morning Thutmose, along with 1,000 men, set off to start working.

As they neared the Sphinx, Thutmose felt a wave of heat surge through his body. He instantly became stronger.

Everyone knew then that Thutmose was the true pharaoh of Egypt, because Harmachis had willed it so.

It took many days to clear away all of the sand from around the statue. But eventually the Sphinx was uncovered.

Thutmose spent three days in prayer at the paws of the Great Sphinx. Then he said to his workers, "Thank you for helping me restore the statue to its glory. Harmachis will surely bless you."

Thutmose placed a giant red granite tablet called a stele between the statue's paws. "This is my Dream Stele," he said. "It tells the story of my vision of Harmachis when I was a prince. And it explains the uncovering of the Great Sphinx of Khafra in the third month of the first year of my reign as pharaoh. It will be left here for all to see."

29

People came and worshipped Harmachis at the Great Sphinx, just as the god wished.

All the statue had foretold came true. Thutmose was blessed with a long, successful rule. He united upper and lower Egypt. He ruled with wisdom, grace, and a happy heart. Even today Thutmose IV is remembered as a great Egyptian pharaoh.

READ MORE

Bell, Michael, and Sarah Quie. *Ancient Egyptian Civilization*. Ancient Civilizations and Their Myths and Legends. New York: Rosen Central, 2010.

Elgin, Kathy. *Egyptian Myths*. Myths From Many Lands. New York: Skyview Books, 2009.

Spengler, Kremena. *Pyramids*. Ancient Egypt. Mankato, Minn.: Capstone Press, 2009.

INTERNET SITES

FactHound offers a safe, fun way to find Internet sites related to this book. All of the sites on FactHound have been researched by our staff.

Here's all you do:

Visit *www.facthound.com*

Type in this code: 9781404871496

 Super-cool stuff! Check out projects, games and lots more at **www.capstonekids.com**

LOOK FOR ALL THE BOOKS IN THE EGYPTIAN MYTHS SERIES:

ISIS AND OSIRIS

ISIS AND THE SEVEN SCORPIONS

THE PRINCE AND THE SPHINX

THE SEARCH FOR THE BOOK OF THOTH

Thanks to our adviser for his expertise and advice:
Terry Flaherty, PhD
Professor of English
Minnesota State University, Mankato

Editor: Shelly Lyons
Designer: Ted Williams
Art Director: Nathan Gassman
Production Specialist: Danielle Ceminsky
The illustrations in this book were created with watercolors, gouache, acrylics, and digitally.
Artistic Effects
Shutterstock: Goran Bogicevic, Kristina Divinchuk, Shvaygert Ekaterina, Vladislav Gurfinkel

Picture Window Books
1710 Roe Crest Drive
North Mankato, MN 56003
www.capstonepub.com

Library of Congress Cataloging-in-Publication Data
Meister, Cari.
 The prince and the sphinx : a retelling / by Cari Meister ; illustrated by Leonardo Meschini.
  p. cm. — (Egyptian myths)
 "A Capstone imprint."
 ISBN 978-1-4048-7149-6 (library binding)
 ISBN 978-1-4048-7242-4 (paperback)
 1. Gods, Egyptian—Juvenile literature. 2. Goddesses, Egyptian—Juvenile literature. 3. Mythology, Egyptian—Juvenile literature. I. Meschini, Leonardo, 1973- II. Title. III. Series: Egyptian myths.
 BL2450.G6M46 2012
 299.3113—dc23
                                2011025842

Printed in the United States of America in Stevens Point, Wisconsin.
102011   006404WZS12